RESILIENCE FOR ACTORS

PSYCHOLOGY FOR ACTORS SERIES

ALEXA ISPAS

WORD
BOTHY

CONTENTS

INTRODUCTION

Life as an actor is full of setbacks.

You must go to one audition after another, for many years, until the right opportunity comes along.

You may also encounter many rejections before getting into drama school, or securing an agent, and face long periods of unemployment.

The good news is that psychology can help you bounce back from all these setbacks instead of sinking into despair.

Over the past few decades, psychologists have uncovered the specific factors that make setbacks particularly painful.

They have also developed a range of tools to

overcome the negative effects that setbacks have on your state of mind.

Using these tools, you will be able to recover quickly and feel motivated to look for new opportunities.

As you will learn throughout this book, resilience is not just about keeping going despite having encountered a setback.

It is about jumping back into action with a positive mindset, to give yourself the best chance of success.

For evolutionary reasons, a setback changes your brain chemistry in a way that makes you hold back from taking action.

These brain chemistry changes deplete you of the energy and motivation to pursue the next opportunity with genuine enthusiasm, until enough time has passed for your brain to rebalance itself.

Repeated setbacks have a cumulative effect, leading to a vicious cycle of despair and ever-decreasing odds of reaching your goals.

The better you understand how a setback affects your state of mind, and the more tools you have to combat its negative effects, the easier and quicker the recovery process will be.

In addition, learning how to skilfully navigate the thoughts and feelings that arise following a setback can insulate you from the cumulative effect of repeated setbacks on your mental health.

I have kept this book short, so you can read it in an afternoon and gain the understanding and practical tools you need to increase your resilience as an actor.

All psychological tools are presented in clear, jargon-free language, and applied specifically to actors, so you will easily understand what to do and be able to use everything you learn straight away.

CHAPTER 1

PURSUING OPPORTUNITIES AS AN ACTOR

OPPORTUNITIES AND EVOLUTION

You have been pursuing opportunities all your life.

As a child, the opportunities you pursued may have been a fun toy or a delicious treat from the sweet shop.

When you decided to become an actor, your opportunity-seeking may have shifted to auditioning for a part, looking for an agent, or applying to drama school.

Seeking such opportunities activates the same brain mechanisms as our ancestors when they were foraging or hunting for prey.

Opportunity-seeking provided our ancestors with a major evolutionary advantage.

Those of our ancestors who went after more opportunities were able to secure more food and better living conditions. They therefore had a better chance of passing on their genes.

As we are the descendants of those who went after more opportunities than their contemporaries, our brain has developed in a way that favors opportunity-seeking.

At a deep level, we equate pursuing an opportunity with meeting our survival needs.

On the other hand, when we encounter a setback in our quest, our brain interprets the situation as a threat to our survival.

DOPAMINE: YOUR BRAIN'S ENERGY BOOSTER

When you pursue an opportunity (e.g., going to an audition), your brain rewards you by releasing dopamine–a so-called "happy chemical" that makes you more energized and motivated than usual.

The bigger the opportunity, the more dopamine your brain releases.

Your brain starts releasing dopamine the moment you become aware of the opportunity, such as when your agent calls to tell you about an audition.

Our ancestors depended on this early dopamine release for their survival.

For example, if one of our ancestors found a river full of fish, this early dopamine release gave them the energy to run back and tell the rest of their people about the river.

Since perceiving something as an opportunity played such a big part in our evolution, your entire body becomes energized as soon as you lock onto your goal.

This is important, because as we will discuss in a later chapter, when your resilience goes down and you get dejected, your openness to see something as an opportunity decreases.

As a result, you will have lower chances of success, leading to a vicious cycle of failure and despair.

CORTISOL: THE HIDDEN ENEMY

Dopamine has an inverse relationship with cortisol, the so-called "stress hormone." When your brain releases dopamine, your cortisol level goes down.

As a result, your immune system and mental

health benefit whenever you experience an increase in dopamine, and suffer when your dopamine comes down and your cortisol rises.

Keeping your cortisol level low through pursuing exciting opportunities is not only good for your acting career; it also helps your overall well-being.

The better you feel, the more fun you are to be around, and the more opportunities you attract into your life.

GETTING CLOSER TO YOUR GOAL

When you pursue an opportunity, your body rewards your efforts with a fresh dopamine boost as you reach every new milestone.

Hearing about an audition, preparing for it, giving a good performance, and receiving a call-back, are all milestones that take you closer to the goal of getting cast and lead to an increase in your energy levels and motivation.

As you complete each of these steps, the rise in dopamine gives you the energy and motivation to push harder towards the finish line.

When the goal comes within reach, your entire

being lights up with the positive expectation of success.

Your body expands, anticipating victory, and you radiate a confident feeling that others can see, which gives them confidence in you.

A setback, such as getting a rejection when you hoped to emerge victorious, interrupts this exhilarating sequence and has a negative effect on your state of mind.

The bigger the dopamine boost you got as you started pursuing the opportunity, the harder this change in brain chemistry will hit you.

Just as there is an evolutionary process for when an opportunity arises and you start pursuing it, there is also a process for when you encounter a setback.

In the next chapter, we will examine this process in detail.

KEY POINTS

- Pursuing an opportunity, such as looking for an agent, auditioning for a role, or applying to drama school, activates the same brain mechanisms as when our ancestors were foraging or hunting for prey.

- When you start seeking such an opportunity, your brain releases dopamine, which gives you extra energy and motivation.

- Dopamine has an inverse relationship with cortisol, the "stress hormone." When dopamine goes up, cortisol comes down, which boosts your immune system and general sense of well-being.

- As you get closer to your goal, your body and mind light up with the positive expectation of success.

- A setback, such as getting a rejection when you hoped to emerge victorious, interrupts this exhilarating sequence and has a negative effect on your state of mind.

CHAPTER 2

SETBACKS AND BRAIN CHEMISTRY

SETBACKS AND DOPAMINE DIPS

When you become aware of an opportunity, your brain releases an initial dopamine burst, which increases your energy levels and motivation.

This initial burst of excitement helps you to start pursuing your goal.

As you get closer to your target, more dopamine becomes available, leading to an exhilarating feel-good effect that makes you increasingly hopeful and confident.

However, when you encounter a setback, all these positive feelings that are the result of dopamine suddenly stop.

Without the energizing effect of dopamine, you feel depleted.

A setback, especially when things have been going well for a while, feels like a punch to the gut.

THAT CORTISOL FEELING

Stopping the flow of dopamine is not the only unpleasant consequence of encountering a setback.

Your body also starts releasing cortisol, the "stress hormone" we discussed in the previous chapter.

While dopamine makes you feel energized and motivated, cortisol makes you anxious and restless, giving you the impression that something is wrong.

It is as if your body is saying, "There is a problem—watch out!".

Indeed, from an evolutionary perspective, encountering a setback seems like a threat to your survival, because the opportunity that might have saved your life is no longer within reach.

As a result, your cortisol rising leads to an uncomfortable feeling in your body which puts you on alert without offering any clear path for resolution.

Because of this sense of danger, you start

paying attention to all the things in your life that worry you and that you had forgotten about while riding high on dopamine.

THE NEGATIVE EFFECT OF ENCOUNTERING A SETBACK

When you encounter a setback, the combination of your dopamine going down and your cortisol rising is designed to hold you back from undertaking any new action until it is safe to do so.

Animals avoid fighting after losing a battle.

Those who go into a fight straight after losing lower their chances of surviving long enough to pass on their genes.

Similarly, when our ancestors encountered a setback, they held back from taking further action until they recovered their energy.

We are the descendants of people who held back when they did not feel energized enough to win.

As a result, encountering a setback changes your brain chemistry in a way that favors holding back.

This change in brain chemistry puts you in a

negative state of mind that is most commonly experienced as a sense of helplessness.

The setback raises the question: if this attempt failed, despite all the effort you put in, why would the next attempt be any more successful?

As an actor, having this question at the back of your mind when going to auditions makes you doubt whether any of your future efforts will be rewarded.

This is likely to affect your motivation to put effort into your next audition and lower the confidence with which you pursue such opportunities.

In the next chapter, we will explore how repeated setbacks can lead to so-called "learned helplessness," a chronic negative state of mind.

However, as you will learn, this dangerous progression from setback to learned helplessness can be prevented if you interpret the setback optimistically.

KEY POINTS

- Encountering a setback stops the dopamine flow. This depletes your energy and deprives you of the exhilarating feeling of moving closer to your goal.

- The energizing influx of dopamine is replaced by an increase in cortisol (the "stress hormone"), which makes you feel anxious and directs your attention to the negative aspects of your life.

- The sudden dip in dopamine, coupled with the rise in cortisol, serves the evolutionary purpose of holding you back from undertaking further action until it is safe to do so.

- This change in your brain chemistry puts you in a negative state of mind, which is commonly described as a feeling of helplessness.

CHAPTER 3

THE RISK OF REPEATED SETBACKS

REPEATED SETBACKS HAVE A CUMULATIVE EFFECT

In the previous chapter, we explored what happens when the exhilarating pursuit of an opportunity, such as auditioning for a desirable part and getting a callback, is interrupted by a setback, such as someone else being cast in the role you were hoping to play.

As your brain chemistry changes through the drop in dopamine and the rise in cortisol, you are likely to feel exhausted and helpless.

In this chapter, we go one step further and explore the effect of repeated setbacks.

Actors must withstand one setback after another before the right opportunity comes along.

If one setback has such a negative impact on your state of mind, what about repeated setbacks?

Evidence suggests that setbacks can have a cumulative effect, gradually leading to a decline in mental health.

REPEATED SETBACKS AND LIFE AS AN ACTOR

Imagine yourself at the beginning of your acting career, full of enthusiasm, ready to take on the world.

Parents and mentors tell you that making a living as an actor is hard and most people fail, but you are determined to prove everybody wrong.

You go to one audition after another, and initially, you take every setback in your stride.

But as the rejections pile up, you become more dejected and begin wondering whether you can make it in this industry.

Soon, these negative thoughts chip away at your self-confidence.

You get more agitated, have trouble sleeping, and your mental health goes into decline.

A sense of desperation works its way into your psyche.

As you start approaching opportunities in this unhealthy way, your lack of self-confidence undermines other people's confidence in you, resulting in ever-decreasing odds of success.

You probably know actors, some of them extremely hard-working and talented, who have gone down this path.

Eventually, they feel so dejected that they stop going to auditions altogether, falling into what Martin Seligman and other psychologists call "learned helplessness," a chronic negative mental state.

When you are in this state of mind, you believe that going to auditions is pointless and will result in failure.

As a result, you stop pursuing opportunities and give up on your acting dream.

On the other hand, you probably also know actors who have kept their spirits up through years of rejections until they got their big break.

These actors illustrate that you can avoid going down the learned helplessness route even after repeated setbacks.

What sets these two groups of actors apart?

The key, as psychological evidence shows, is interpreting setbacks in an optimistic way.

PESSIMISM AND MENTAL HEALTH

Resilience is not just about jumping back into action following a setback.

It is about interpreting the setback optimistically, so you can pursue the next opportunity with a healthy mindset.

The mistake many actors make when they experience repeated rejections is to fall into a pessimistic mindset.

It makes sense why they would do so–they are trying to avoid the pain of further disappointments.

The problem is that when you interpret setbacks pessimistically, you deplete yourself of dopamine and it takes longer to recover.

As pessimism reduces your openness to see something as an opportunity, you end up going after fewer opportunities and do so with less motivation, which lowers your chances of success.

By contrast, when you interpret the setback optimistically, you feel motivated to look for new opportunities, which boosts your dopamine.

This increases your energy levels and you once again feel enthusiastic and motivated.

In addition, when you find your next opportunity, you stand a good chance of success, because the increase in dopamine makes you radiate confidence and positivity.

Research by Martin Seligman and his colleagues shows that the more you think like an optimist, the quicker and easier you can get over any setback, which increases your chances of future success.

THE POSITIVE FEEDBACK LOOP OF OPTIMISM

Seeking and pursuing an opportunity is energizing and motivating, creating a positive feedback loop.

To set this positive feedback loop into motion, you must believe it is possible to reach your goal. This means you must be in an optimistic rather than a pessimistic mindset.

The more you seek and pursue opportunities, the more energized and motivated you become, which gives you the energy and motivation to go after more opportunities.

Interpreting setbacks optimistically is especially important for actors, because it helps minimize the cumulative negative effect of repeated setbacks.

Psychological research shows that even when faced with repeated setbacks, optimists avoid the vicious cycle of declining mental health that pessimists fall into.

In the next chapter, you will learn about three criteria you can use to distinguish between an optimistic and a pessimistic interpretation of encountering a setback.

KEY POINTS

- Evidence suggests that repeated setbacks can have a cumulative effect.
- The disappointment of pursuing a string of opportunities that do not materialize leads many actors to adopt a pessimistic outlook. This sets in motion a vicious cycle of decreasing odds of success and declining mental health.
- To avoid going down this path, you need to learn to view every setback with optimism rather than pessimism.

- Optimism helps you overcome the setback and go after new opportunities with a healthy mindset, while pessimism makes it hard to heal from the hurt and puts your mental health at risk.
- Psychological evidence shows that even when faced with repeated setbacks, optimists avoid the vicious cycle of declining mental health that pessimists fall into.

CHAPTER 4

THE HIDDEN COST OF PESSIMISM

HOW TO AVOID PESSIMISM

In the previous chapter, we saw how repeated setbacks can have a cumulative effect, leading to a slippery slope of declining mental health.

Actors are particularly at risk of this, as they must endure years of rejection before the right opportunities come along.

In this chapter, you will learn how to avoid going down this path if you are faced with repeated setbacks.

As psychological studies show, the way to increase your resilience is to get into the habit of interpreting setbacks with optimism rather than pessimism.

Optimism helps you overcome setbacks and go after new opportunities with a healthy mindset.

By contrast, pessimism puts your mental health at risk by allowing repeated setbacks to have a negative impact on your state of mind.

THREE ASPECTS OF PESSIMISTIC THINKING

Psychological studies by Martin Seligman and colleagues have identified three key aspects that characterize pessimistic thinking: "permanence," "pervasiveness," and "personalization."

"Permanence" refers to the pessimistic tendency to see the effects of a setback as permanent, or–in the case of actors–to believe that finding success may never happen.

By contrast, optimistic actors believe their lack of success is only temporary.

"Pervasiveness," the second aspect, refers to the pessimistic tendency to see a setback in one area of life, such as one's career, as also affecting other areas, such as one's relationships.

Optimists, on the other hand, see the setback as only affecting the area of life in which it occurred, which means they can still enjoy other areas of their life.

The third aspect, "personalization," refers to the pessimistic tendency to see oneself as having caused the setback, for example, by having made bad choices during an audition.

Optimists, on the other hand, see the setback as the result of outside circumstances.

PESSIMISM AS CHANGEABLE PATTERNS OF THOUGHT

Although people may identify as an "optimist" or a "pessimist," or be seen as such by others, optimism and pessimism are changeable patterns of thought rather than fixed personality traits.

Because of the changeable nature of these patterns, you can learn new ways of thinking.

In addition, we all differ in the extent to which we think optimistically or pessimistically about each of the three aspects of pessimism.

Even if you identify as an optimist, you can have certain patterns of thought that are pessimistic.

For example, you could see setbacks optimistically regarding the permanence or pervasiveness aspect, but beat yourself up over mistakes you made, which you see as the cause of the setback.

This would mean you think pessimistically when it comes to the personalization aspect.

LEARNED OPTIMISM

If you are not a natural optimist, or have a tendency towards pessimism in relation to certain aspects, you can retrain your thinking through a process Martin Seligman called "learned optimism."

This process provides a set of tools through which you can learn to think of the setback as temporary, restricted to the specific area of life where it occurred, and caused by circumstances outside your control.

Even if you find yourself in the "optimism" camp most of the time, you can use learned optimism to identify any pessimistic patterns of thought you may have.

Learning how to interpret setbacks optimistically rather than pessimistically is especially important for actors, as it helps overcome the cumulative effect of repeated setbacks.

In the next chapter, we will examine the first stage in the process of learned optimism: how to identify your habitual pessimistic thoughts.

- Psychologists have identified three key aspects that distinguish optimistic from pessimistic thinking in relation to setbacks.
- Optimists and pessimists differ in their estimation of how long setbacks will keep happening, how much of their life the setback will affect, and the reason for the setback.
- For optimists, the setback is temporary, confined to one area of life, and due to outside circumstances.
- For pessimists, setbacks will keep happening for a long time, undermine everything else in their life, and are their own fault.
- If you are not a natural optimist, you can learn to let go of your pessimistic thought patterns through a process called "learned optimism."
- Even if you interpret setbacks optimistically most of the time, you can use learned optimism to change the pessimistic thought patterns you may

have in certain circumstances, or in relation to one or more of the three aspects of pessimism.

CHAPTER 5

THE OPTIMISM PATH

FIRST STEPS IN LEARNED OPTIMISM

Learned optimism is based on the premise that optimism is not a fixed trait but a set of habitual patterns of thought, which means you can learn to think optimistically.

Doing so will make it easier and quicker to overcome any setback you encounter.

For actors, thinking optimistically despite encountering numerous setbacks is a particularly valuable skill to learn.

By retraining your thinking, you can avoid a decline in your mental health when facing repeated setbacks.

In this chapter, we will focus on the first step in

changing your thought patterns: identifying your pessimistic thoughts as they arise.

NOTICING YOUR THOUGHTS

When you encounter a setback, you immediately have a series of thoughts relating to how the setback will affect you and the reasons it happened.

These thoughts come so quickly that you may have never taken the time to examine them in detail, yet they are worth paying attention to.

The thoughts you have when you encounter a setback influence how you feel and the actions you take.

As a result, they influence how quickly you can overcome the setback.

If your thoughts are optimistic, they can help you recover from the hurt generated by the setback, motivating you to look for new opportunities.

By contrast, if your thoughts are pessimistic, they make you feel even worse, which means you will need longer to recover.

Over time, experiencing repeated setbacks may lead to a decline in your mental health.

The first step in the process of learned optimism is to get into the habit of noticing your pessimistic thoughts as they arise.

Over the next few days or weeks, take some time to reflect on your thoughts relating to the setbacks you have experienced recently.

How many of these thoughts make the setbacks seem never-ending, affecting the whole of your life, or caused by your own mistakes?

As you start paying attention to your thoughts, you will notice certain tendencies.

For example, you may find optimistic patterns in your thinking about one of the three aspects, but pessimistic patterns in relation to another.

In examining your thoughts, you must adopt a non-judgmental attitude.

You are simply taking note of your thoughts; the purpose of this exercise is to observe your existing patterns, not to make yourself feel bad.

HOW TO IDENTIFY PESSIMISTIC THOUGHTS

How can you tell whether your thoughts are optimistic or pessimistic?

When assessed along the three aspects of permanence, pervasiveness, and personalization, the words you use to describe the setback to yourself and others will give you clues.

A pessimistic interpretation is characterized by describing the setback as never-ending, affecting all areas of your life, and/or caused by something you did.

By contrast, when your thoughts are optimistic, you describe the setback as temporary, only affecting a small area of your life, and due to outside circumstances.

Another way to identify pessimistic thoughts is by how they make you feel.

Pessimistic thoughts lead to feeling powerless and wanting to give up, whereas optimistic thoughts are energizing and motivate you to look for new opportunities.

In the next chapter, you will learn a set of tools you can use to challenge your pessimistic thoughts and shift your perspective towards optimism.

KEY POINTS

- The first step in the "learned optimism" process is to identify your pessimistic thoughts by examining what you say to yourself and others following a setback.

- How you describe the setback gives you clues whether you are viewing it optimistically or pessimistically.

- When you view the setback optimistically, you see it as temporary, only affecting a small area of your life, and due to outside circumstances.

- Pessimistic thoughts are characterized by seeing the setback as never-ending, affecting all areas of your life, and/or caused by something you did.

- Your thoughts influence your feelings and subsequent actions.

- When you describe the setback optimistically, you become energized and motivated to look for new opportunities.

- By contrast, describing the setback in a pessimistic way depletes you of energy and motivation.

- As you start paying attention to your thoughts, you may find optimistic patterns about one of the three aspects and pessimistic patterns in relation to another.

- Adopt a non-judgmental attitude while examining your thoughts and taking note of your tendencies.

CHAPTER 6

TOOLS TO COMBAT PESSIMISM

CHANGING PESSIMISTIC THOUGHTS

In the previous chapter, we discussed the first part of the learned optimism process: how to identify your pessimistic thoughts.

In this chapter, we will explore the second part of this process, which involves learning a set of tools that will shift your pessimistic thoughts towards optimism.

The more skilled you become at using these tools, the easier it will be to recover from setbacks and feel motivated to start looking for new opportunities.

LEARNED OPTIMISM TOOLS

Ask yourself for evidence

The most obvious way to challenge a pessimistic thought is to ask yourself if there is any evidence to support it.

Pessimistic thoughts are often caused by your low mood. It is therefore likely that when you start looking for evidence, you won't find any.

Recognizing this lack of evidence will make it easier to challenge your pessimistic thoughts and start thinking optimistically.

For example, let's say you are thinking, "I will never make it as an actor."

Perhaps this thought goes through your mind every time you encounter a setback in your acting career.

What evidence do you have to back up this pessimistic thought?

You can probably think of many actors who experienced one rejection after another until they found success in their profession.

Can you know for sure this will not happen to you?

Once you realize there is no evidence to support your pessimistic thought, it becomes easier to change it into a more positive evaluation, such as, "This opportunity wasn't meant to be, but my big break will come soon."

This alternative is more motivating and energizing than your initial reaction.

As such, it helps you overcome the hurt and start looking for new opportunities, instead of wallowing in hopelessness and despair.

Reframe the setback

If you find evidence supporting your pessimistic thoughts, another way to stimulate optimistic thinking is to reframe your thoughts into alternative, optimistic scenarios.

For example, let's say your pessimistic thoughts relate to negative consequences that may arise because of the setback.

However, the setback is likely to have many potential consequences, some of which may be positive. Focusing on these positive alternatives is energizing and motivating.

As you encounter a setback, get into the habit of asking yourself what positive consequences could come from it.

When first applying this tool, you may think of

positive consequences you may not believe will come true, such as, "Something better may be just around the corner."

If this is the case, remember that much of pessimist thinking consists of the reverse, which is to latch on to the most disastrous future possibilities because they resonate with your low mood.

De-catastrophize your thoughts

As you start noticing what you habitually say to yourself following a setback, you may realize that your pessimistic thoughts have a tendency towards exaggeration, making the setback seem catastrophic.

Pessimistic thinking highlights the worst potential consequences arising from a setback, which are the most permanent, pervasive, and personal, as these are the ones that resonate with your low mood.

Upon closer examination, are your prospects following the setback as disastrous as your pessimistic mindset encourages you to believe?

What evidence do you have that the implications are as awful as your pessimistic thinking suggests?

Once you look for actual evidence that would support your catastrophizing thoughts, you are unlikely to find any.

Use this lack of evidence as motivation to come up with more optimistic alternatives.

Examine the usefulness of your thoughts

One of the easiest ways to challenge your pessimistic thoughts is based on their (lack of) usefulness.

Thinking pessimistically about a setback makes you feel even worse, whereas thinking optimistically about it re-energizes you and lifts your mood.

When you find yourself weighed down by pessimistic thoughts, ask yourself how thinking in this way is of any use.

Becoming clear on how little such thoughts serve you will motivate you to shift your perspective towards optimism.

The goal is to direct your attention to energizing thoughts that help you recover from the setback and motivate you to look for new opportunities.

Distract yourself

Distracting yourself is a great strategy when pessimistic thoughts about the setback keep running through your mind, despite your best efforts.

You may also want to use distraction once you have successfully challenged your pessimistic thoughts with some of the other tools, to allow your mind to focus elsewhere.

To distract yourself, redirect your attention away from the setback and towards something more interesting and enjoyable.

The easier it is to distract yourself, the closer you are to moving on from the pain of the setback and becoming interested in new opportunities.

Initiate change

In most cases, your pessimistic thoughts are distortions caused by changes in brain chemistry and your resulting low mood.

The best way to deal with them is to challenge them, reframe them, distract yourself from them— do anything that will prevent them from affecting your state of mind and your chances of future success.

However, if your interpretation of the setback turns out to be accurate, using the mindset tools you have just learned is not enough; you need to change the underlying reality of your situation.

In such cases, focus on what changes you can make in your life.

Even if your pessimistic assessment is true now, you can create better circumstances for the future.

The shift in focus from a pessimistic assessment of a setback to asking yourself how to improve your existing situation is empowering.

Instead of dwelling on the problems, your mind starts looking for potential solutions.

As this search represents a desirable goal, your new focus will lift your mood by boosting your dopamine and lowering your cortisol.

APPLYING LEARNED OPTIMISM TOOLS

The tools in this chapter take a while to learn and practice.

However, dismantling your habitual pessimistic thoughts is worth the effort.

Doing so will protect your mental health and improve your odds of future success.

By providing you with ways to change your pessimistic thoughts into optimistic ones, the tools help you shift your feelings from despair to hope.

This means you will need less time to recover from setbacks and will find it easier to open yourself up to new opportunities.

Which tool is the most effective depends on the situation you find yourself in and the specific thoughts running through your mind.

Initially, I advise you to go through all of these tools any time you identify a pessimistic thought, as each can help you in a different way.

You will soon get a sense of how to use these tools in practice and the benefits each of them brings.

Over time, you will probably develop a preference for some tools over others.

For example, if your pessimistic thoughts have a catastrophizing tendency, you may find the de-catastrophizing tool particularly effective.

Over the next three chapters, we will return to the aspects of pessimistic thinking we discussed in chapter 4: permanence, pervasiveness, and personalization.

We will examine in detail how to apply each

learned optimism tool to thoughts relating to these three aspects.

The next chapter will focus on applying the tools to pessimistic thoughts relating to the permanence aspect.

KEY POINTS

- Once you identify a pessimistic thought, the next step is to decide how best to change it into an optimistic one.
- You can shift your pessimistic thoughts towards optimism based on lack of evidence, or reframe them into a more optimistic alternative.
- You can also challenge them based on being too extreme, or unhelpful and disempowering.
- While changing your pessimistic thought patterns, you may also want to distract yourself from your thoughts.
- If you find that some of your pessimistic thoughts are realistic, you can make changes to create the right circumstances for optimistic thinking.

CHAPTER 7

ACTORS AND FUTURE EXPECTATIONS

TIME-RELATED PESSIMISTIC BELIEFS

In this chapter, you will learn how to deal with pessimistic thoughts related to the "permanence" aspect, such as estimations of how long it will take to find success.

As previously mentioned, optimists believe the setback is temporary and success is just around the corner.

By contrast, pessimists believe the setback or lack of success will be permanent.

The goal is to get into the habit of seeing setbacks in your acting career as temporary.

By interpreting setbacks optimistically, you are motivating yourself to look for new opportunities.

This will replenish your dopamine and prevent cortisol from dragging down your mood.

In addition, because of the dopamine, you will have the energy to approach the next challenge with good chances of success.

"HOW LONG WILL IT TAKE" QUESTIONS

"How long before I get my foot in the door?"

"How many auditions before I get cast?"

"How many years before I achieve success?"

These are a few of the questions you may ask yourself after encountering a setback, for example, when you don't get a callback after a particularly promising audition.

A pessimistic thought might sound like, "I will never achieve success."

Can you see how demotivating such a thought is?

If you believe your efforts will never pay off, the negative feelings associated with the setback will only get worse.

As a result, you will not be motivated to find another opportunity, and even when an opportunity comes your way, you may not recognize it as such.

This sets in motion the negative path we have discussed in a previous chapter, where you don't replenish your dopamine and your cortisol rises even higher, making it harder to overcome the setback.

If you don't seek, you don't find, so your odds of success decrease. Over time, it becomes easy to sink into despair.

By contrast, identifying your thoughts as pessimistic and deciding to challenge them gives you a chance to increase your resilience.

Instead of allowing your pessimistic thoughts to make you feel worse, you can turn these difficult time-related questions into fresh fuel for your optimism, energy, and motivation.

There is no way of knowing how long things will take, because you cannot predict the future; all you can do is guess.

You can either tell yourself something that makes you feel even worse or you can tell yourself something empowering, that lifts you out of your negative mental state and energizes you.

If you must guess anyway, why not tell yourself something that helps you recover and makes you feel good?

For example, you could describe the setback in

temporary terms, such as, "Success is just around the corner."

Optimistic self-talk motivates you to try again, with confidence and enthusiasm.

By thinking of the setback as temporary, you are helping yourself heal from the emotional pain associated with the setback and motivating yourself to look for your next opportunity.

As the act of seeking releases more dopamine, you are supplying yourself with extra energy, which increases your chances of success.

In addition, the feel-good effect of dopamine lowers the cortisol generated by the setback.

Soon, you become so engrossed in pursuing the next opportunity that you forget about this setback.

Let us see how you can use each of the tools you learned in the previous chapter to counteract your pessimistic thoughts relating to the permanence aspect of pessimism.

ASK YOURSELF FOR EVIDENCE

When you encounter a setback, notice your pessimistic thoughts relating to the permanence aspect.

Are these thoughts supported by any evidence?

For example, right after the setback, you may think, "Things will never get better for me."

Is there any evidence that supports this thought? How can you know what will happen in the future?

In fact, once you examine these kinds of thoughts more closely, you are likely to come across evidence that counters your pessimism.

We have all heard of actors who were struggling and were ready to give up when suddenly their big break came and everything changed.

Can you be certain this will not happen to you? What if your big break came with your next audition?

The only way to find out is to look for the next opportunity, instead of allowing this setback to drag you into sadness and despair.

REFRAME THE SETBACK

If you find evidence that supports your pessimistic thoughts, another strategy is to reframe how you view the setback.

There are several good ways to reframe your pessimistic thoughts relating to the permanence aspect.

Focus on the familiarity effect

One of the easiest ways to reframe your pessimistic thoughts is to take a broad view of what constitutes "success" in particular situations, such as going to an audition.

Many actors see the end goal of an audition as getting the part.

The problem is that the likelihood of being cast is small, which means the odds of encountering a setback are high.

What if you chose a different goal instead, one that would make it easier to interpret the outcome optimistically even if you did not get the part?

For example, what if you defined your goal as giving a good performance during the audition?

In that case, not getting the part would not constitute a setback, as long as you gave a good performance.

If this possibility appeals to you, it is worth knowing about what psychologists call the "familiarity effect," which can be summed up as, "The more they see you, the more they like you."

To benefit from the familiarity effect, don't treat any audition as a one-off.

Use your performance as an opportunity to

provide the casting team with a taste of what you can offer as an actor.

If industry professionals keep seeing you in auditions and you consistently deliver good performances, you will become someone they will think of for a variety of future opportunities.

The members of the casting team are in this industry for the long haul, and so are you.

Focus on giving a good performance and forget about the outcome.

Set a rejection target

Setting a rejection target is another helpful way to reframe your pessimistic thoughts, especially when it comes to auditions.

As you are likely to get many rejections anyway, why not give yourself a yearly (or even a monthly) rejection target?

Instead of seeing rejections as failures, give yourself a rejection target.

In doing so, you are setting yourself up for a situation where you cannot fail.

If you get a callback, that is a win, because you are getting closer to getting cast.

But if you don't hear back, you are one step

closer to reaching your rejection target, so you win anyway.

In this way, rejections become something to be celebrated.

With every rejection, you are getting one step closer to reaching your target.

By turning rejections into a game you put yourself in control, instead of allowing rejections to get you down.

As finding the right part is often a numbers game, this strategy will work wonders for your acting career and your mindset.

In addition, approaching auditions with this win-no-matter-what attitude makes it easier to benefit from the "familiarity effect," setting yourself up for future success.

DE-CATASTROPHIZE YOUR THOUGHTS

Another way to change your pessimistic thoughts relating to the permanence aspect is to notice any tendency to exaggerate the setback's negative implications.

One clue your pessimistic thoughts tend towards catastrophizing is if you use words such as "always," or "never," in a pessimistic context.

For example, let's say you notice saying to yourself, following a setback, "I will never make it as an actor."

This leads to a feeling of hopelessness, which means it will take longer to regain your energy and motivation.

If you notice such thoughts, it is time to de-catastrophize your thinking.

Looking at things objectively, is the situation that bad? Do you truly believe this pessimistic assessment of your future chances?

Maybe it will take you one or two years longer than you expected to get into drama school, secure an agent, or book your first acting job.

You may have to be more patient than you had expected, but that is not as bad as the word "never" seems to suggest.

Besides–to use reframing once more–maybe having more time to develop as an actor before your big break comes is a blessing in disguise.

Things change quickly once the right opportunity comes along.

You won't have as much time to try different things and learn what works best.

Whereas at this moment in your career, you

can take your time to develop both in terms of your craft and on a personal level.

By approaching the waiting period as an opportunity for growth, you are increasing your resilience.

In addition, you are making sure that when your big break comes, you will make the most of it.

EXAMINE THE USEFULNESS OF YOUR THOUGHTS

Another great way to challenge your pessimistic thoughts relating to the permanence aspect is to realize how unhelpful these thoughts are.

Consider the following: thinking that success is just around the corner is energizing.

By contrast, thinking you may never find success is demotivating.

You cannot know for sure what will happen when you go after your next opportunity.

Why not focus on the possibility that success may come soon?

Doing so will motivate you to approach your next opportunity with confidence, which increases your chances of success.

DISTRACT YOURSELF

Maybe you have already tried all the previous tools and you are still pessimistic about how long things will take.

Sometimes these tools work to some extent, but you still come across pessimistic thoughts that trigger your helplessness.

In that case, try distracting yourself.

The easiest way to do so when dealing with permanence-related pessimistic thoughts is to give yourself a quick and easy goal.

Working towards this goal will satisfy your urge to bring something to successful completion.

Set an easily achievable goal

Give yourself something positive to focus on: an easily achievable goal, something you can complete quickly, within a day or a week.

The goal does not need to be acting-related.

It can be anything that feels meaningful to you, such as cooking a delicious meal you have never tried before.

Completing a goal releases dopamine. This

makes it easier to distract yourself from the setback and find a new source of joy.

This increase in dopamine will make it easier to think optimistically, giving you the motivation to look for new opportunities.

INITIATE CHANGE

What if, while going through the previous tools, you realize that your pessimistic evaluation of the future is realistic?

For example, your agent may not call often, or you may not have an agent.

This means that if you go to one audition and don't get a callback, your next opportunity is unlikely to come soon, giving your pessimistic thoughts strength.

Alternatively, you may live in an area where there are not many auditions.

That also makes every setback feel worse, because again, you know it will be a while before another opportunity comes along.

Even though nowadays you can often audition through a self-tape instead of turning up in person, living in a remote area may still make it difficult to network with industry professionals and find out about relevant auditions.

In such situations, the way to think optimistically is to focus on what you can change about your current circumstances.

For example, you might look for another agent, if you have good reason to believe you could get better representation elsewhere.

You may also want to consider moving to a different location, where there are more acting-related opportunities.

If neither of these changes is possible, don't just rely on auditions. Make your own work.

Even if you live in a small place where not much is happening on the acting front, the internet provides many possibilities for performing in front of an international audience.

This will give you a guaranteed way to regularly replenish your dopamine, making it easier to overcome any setbacks relating to auditions.

In addition, look for other sources of accomplishment in your life, besides acting.

These other sources do not need to be career-related, as long as they energize and motivate you.

Introducing novelty into your life is another

great way to encourage your brain to release dopamine, thereby lowering your cortisol.

Start something new. Learn something new. Meet someone new. Look for new opportunities.

Even changing your hair color or clothing style are great ways to increase your dopamine, so make sure you regularly bring new things into your life.

The more you get used to creating circumstances that nurture optimistic thinking, the easier it will be to recover from setbacks.

KEY POINTS

- It is natural, after a setback, to ask yourself how long it will take for your efforts to pay off, but there is no way to answer this question accurately.
- What you tell yourself will either make you feel worse or replenish your energy and motivation.
- If you think pessimistically about how long it will take to find success, challenge your thinking. Many actors struggle for some time before finding the right opportunity, but things turn around quickly when it finally comes.

- You can also use the so-called "familiarity effect" to reframe every audition as building working relationships with industry professionals. In addition, set a yearly rejection target, which will allow you to see every rejection as a win.

- You may also need to de-catastrophize your thoughts about how long it will take to succeed, and question the usefulness of such thoughts.

- If you need to distract yourself from your pessimistic thoughts relating to time, you can do so by setting and completing an easily achievable goal.

- You may also need to initiate changes in your life that will make it easier to have an optimistic outlook following a setback.

CHAPTER 8

ACTORS AND LIVING A BALANCED LIFE

KEEPING THE SETBACK CONTAINED

When you view an acting career setback through the pessimistic lens, you are likely to believe that this setback will affect many or even all areas of your life.

This includes elements of your life not related to acting, such as your relationships and your ability to support yourself financially.

By contrast, those with an optimistic mindset keep the setback confined to the area of life in which it occurred.

In this chapter, we will apply learned optimism to pessimistic thoughts you may have about how a setback in your acting career will affect the rest of your life.

The goal is to make sure that setbacks in your acting career do not spill over and impact other areas.

If you keep your setbacks confined to your acting career, you can draw strength from other areas of your life while you recover.

This will help you process your disappointment quicker and give you the energy to go after new opportunities.

FINDING BALANCE

Are you perhaps so identified with being an actor that you forget to find joy in other areas of your life?

The more you fall into the trap of allowing your acting ambitions to define you as a person, the more you put yourself at risk of pessimistic thinking.

When you encounter a setback in your acting career, you are likely to feel that your whole life is shot to pieces. Everything feels tainted by a sense of contagion.

Thoughts such as, "My life is ruined," and,

"Everything is falling apart," are symptoms of this type of pessimistic thinking and put you at risk of developing mental health problems.

Thinking that your whole life will be affected by the setback makes it difficult to find healthy sources of dopamine that could help you recover.

The good news is that you can avoid this situation by learning to take charge of your thinking.

Optimistic thinking involves seeing the big picture, of which your acting career is only one part.

When you encounter a setback in your acting career, optimism will shift your attention to areas of your life where things are going well, allowing you to draw strength from those areas.

This will make it easier and quicker to recover from any acting career setback.

You will soon feel motivated to go after the next opportunity with your self-confidence restored.

ASK YOURSELF FOR EVIDENCE

When you notice pessimistic thoughts such as, "My life is ruined," going through your mind, ask yourself whether this is true.

If you spend some time considering the evidence for such thoughts, you will soon discover areas of your life where things are going well.

This is great news, because you now have a source of joy you can use to recover from the setback.

Soon enough, the positive feelings associated with these other areas will allow you to replenish your dopamine and start looking for new opportunities.

REFRAME THE SETBACK

Let's say that when you look for evidence, you find that many areas of your life have been affected; it is not just a matter of being pessimistic.

This may be the case if, for example, you get fired from a long-term acting job, such as a TV series where you had been part of the main cast.

In this type of scenario, the setback may also have a negative impact on your finances and isolate you from your current social circle.

If you find yourself in this kind of situation, the way to change your pessimistic outlook into optimism is captured by the well-known saying, "As one door closes, another one opens."

What if this setback is a blessing in disguise, leading to a change in direction?

Maybe your life as you know it is indeed over, but a new and exciting chapter is about to begin.

Even just considering this possibility is energizing and motivating.

Wondering about this new direction will encourage your brain to release dopamine, supplying you with extra energy and making it easier to recover from the setback.

Once you see the setback in this positive light, you will find it easier to bounce back and look for new opportunities.

DE-CATASTROPHIZE YOUR THOUGHTS

If you have extremely pessimistic thoughts, such as, "My life is ruined," following a setback, ask yourself if there is a less destructive way to view the situation.

The "identity circle" will help you reflect on this question optimistically and keep any acting career setback in perspective.

The identity circle

The "identity circle," inspired by Dan Siegel's more complex "wheel of awareness," is a simple tool you can use to gain some perspective on the importance of acting in your life.

Imagine yourself in the center of a circle, with everything that is important to you represented as points on the edge.

Your identity as an actor represents one of these points, but as you look at this circle, you can also see many other points from your place in the center.

There is your identity when you go to a bill-paying job you might have, your identity as someone's friend, and any other identities that make up who you are as a person.

From your place in the center, you can see the whole picture.

Your identity as an actor means a lot to you, but it is not the whole of who you are.

Thinking of yourself in this way reminds you not to get fixated on this one identity.

When you encounter an acting-related setback, you can use your other identities to find joy, which your acting career cannot offer at that moment.

Doing so will make it easier and quicker to overcome the setback.

If, while using this tool, you realize you are so deeply identified with being an actor you rarely think of yourself in any other way, then perhaps this is the time to reflect on other aspects of yourself that are important to you.

That way, when your acting career is not going well, you will have other ways to maintain a strong sense of self.

EXAMINE THE USEFULNESS OF YOUR THOUGHTS

Another way to counteract your pessimism is to ask yourself, what is the use in thinking this way?

Thinking that your whole life is ruined only makes you feel worse.

It depletes you of energy and insulates you from areas of your life that bring you joy.

This kind of thinking is toxic; it is a waste of your time and energy.

Why not consider how the setback could be a blessing in disguise?

You could also de-catastrophize your thoughts

by acknowledging other areas of your life besides acting that bring you joy.

Both strategies will inspire you to look for something positive–other opportunities or aspects of yourself that you may have neglected.

Using these simple mindset hacks, you can shift your attention away from your pessimistic thoughts.

DISTRACT YOURSELF

If you find that, despite using these other tools, you still feel pessimistic about how non-acting areas of your life are affected by the setback, it is time to distract yourself.

Do something unrelated to acting that brings you pleasure and feeds your soul.

Drawing fresh energy and meaning from this activity will make it quicker and easier to recover from the setback.

Don't attempt to distract yourself with anything unhealthy, such as alcohol, drugs, or junk food.

Although these can temporarily improve your mood, they have negative long-term consequences.

It may be difficult to distract yourself if acting

is your main source of joy, but in the spirit of reframing, this is your opportunity to introduce new things into your life.

In this way, you are proving to yourself that you can find activities other than acting that bring you pleasure.

INITIATE CHANGE

While going through the previous tools, you may find that the setback has indeed affected your whole life; it is not just a matter of pessimism.

This is more likely in certain circumstances, for instance, if your only sense of meaning comes from acting.

You may also be more prone to this type of pessimistic thinking if most of your friends are actors, or if you are in a relationship with another actor.

If this is the case, overcoming this setback is not just a matter of changing the way you view it, from pessimism to optimism; you may also need to make big changes in your life.

Take time for self-care, widen your circle of friends, and find additional sources of joy in your life besides acting.

By making space in your life for non-acting pursuits, you are improving your ability to overcome future setbacks.

KEY POINTS

- When you are in a pessimistic mindset, you may overestimate the extent to which a setback in your acting career will affect the rest of your life.
- You may feel that the setback has affected everything, but usually, this is a perception you can change by reminding yourself of all the good things in your life.
- If the setback has affected your whole life, you may need to make certain changes to create better circumstances for optimism.
- This may include widening your circle of friends and finding other sources of enjoyment besides acting.

CHAPTER 9

ACTORS AND SELF-BLAME

PESSIMISM AND SELF-BLAME

When you encounter a setback in your acting
career, do you blame yourself, or outside circumstances?

When you view an acting career setback
through the pessimistic lens, you are likely to
believe there is something you could have done
differently.

This train of thought makes you fall into so-
called "rumination."

You keep replaying the situation in your head,
imagining a more positive outcome if you had
made different choices.

By contrast, optimists see setbacks as being

caused by outside circumstances, and therefore avoid falling into the rumination trap.

Although blaming outside circumstances may sound like avoiding responsibility for your mistakes, evidence shows that pessimists tend to overestimate the extent to which their actions caused the setback to happen.

This self-blaming tendency makes them feel even worse. As a result, it takes them longer to recover from the setback and look for new opportunities.

In this chapter, we will apply the learned optimism tools to change any self-blaming thoughts you may have regarding the setbacks you encounter.

The goal is to make it easier to overcome your setbacks by avoiding unnecessary self-blame.

SETBACKS ARE NOT YOUR FAULT

"Could I have gotten the part, had I made different choices?"

"Did I mess up this opportunity?"

"What did I do wrong?"

What you tell yourself when these kinds of questions come into your mind has a powerful impact on how quickly you can overcome the setback.

Blaming yourself for the setback will make you feel worse.

As a result, it will take longer to heal from the hurt than if you see the setback as having been caused by outside circumstances.

You may find this denial of responsibility controversial. After all, should we not take responsibility for our mistakes?

The problem is that, in most cases, there is no way to know whether something you perceive as a mistake was indeed the reason for the setback.

It is far more likely that the reason you were not chosen for the part, or did not get into drama school, or did not secure the agent of your dreams, is that you were not the right person for that particular opportunity.

There was nothing you could have done to change the outcome.

Secondly, when you are in a pessimistic state of mind, you are likely to do more than take note of your mistakes.

Instead, you are likely to think so badly of yourself that it becomes paralyzing, making the setback more impactful than it already is.

Studies show that pessimists overestimate the extent to which they are responsible for their setbacks.

Instead of simply noting something that went wrong so they can avoid making the same mistake in the future, they fall into the rumination trap.

The ability to self-reflect is amazing, but it must be contained, or it will take over your life.

Slipping into rumination is a recipe for disaster.

The harder you are on yourself, analyzing the situation over and over, the more cortisol you produce.

You are eventually so weighed down by your self-judgments that it becomes difficult to get yourself out of this mindset.

By turning an overly critical eye on yourself, you become your biggest enemy.

If you are prone to rumination, a potentially minor setback can turn into an enormous drain on your self-confidence.

This may lead to long-term problems for both your career and your mental health.

As such, it is better to err on the side of blaming any acting career setbacks on outside circumstances.

ASK YOURSELF FOR EVIDENCE

The easiest way to change self-blaming thoughts, such as, "I messed up this opportunity," into optimistic ones, is to ask yourself if there is any evidence that would support your pessimistic interpretation.

In most cases, you don't know the reason you were not chosen for something.

If there is no evidence that the setback was caused by something you did, why blame yourself and feel even worse?

What you need after encountering a setback is the opposite of self-blame; you need a self-confidence boost. The next tool will help with that.

Your greatest hits

Your "greatest hits" are moments in your life when you felt successful and accomplished.

Make a list of any such times you can think of.

Acknowledge times when you were especially creative or clever, as well as moments when you realized you had improved as an actor or that made you a more rounded human being.

Put this list somewhere you can easily access,

and whenever you have self-blaming thoughts, read this list.

Make sure to read each item slowly. Give yourself time to remember all the sensory details of the moments you have listed.

Reading and re-reading this list following a setback will make you feel better about yourself.

This will speed up your recovery and allow you to jump back into action with a healthy mindset.

REFRAME THE SETBACK

If there is something that you wish you could have done differently, the best way to deal with self-blaming thoughts is to reframe the experience as a learning opportunity.

The next tool will help you reframe your pessimistic thoughts into optimistic ones.

The growth mindset

The "growth mindset," a term coined by Carol Dweck, refers to a way of approaching learning that sees mistakes as a starting point for making progress.

When you adopt a growth mindset, any mistakes you make become learning opportunities.

Instead of beating yourself up when you realize you made a mistake, the growth mindset encourages you to delight in the fact that you now know something you did not know before.

In contrast to the "growth mindset" stands what Carol Dweck calls the "fixed mindset," which assumes that our abilities, character, and intelligence, are inborn traits that cannot meaningfully change through effort.

When you see mistakes from the fixed mindset perspective, your self-confidence is likely to suffer, because this mindset steers you towards a critical view of yourself.

If you are faced with a setback where you wish you could have done things differently, embracing the growth mindset will allow you to view any mistake with optimism.

Instead of criticizing yourself, you take note of what you could have done differently and make sure to avoid making the same mistake in the future.

This will help you avoid falling into the rumination trap and motivate you to look for new opportunities.

DE-CATASTROPHIZE YOUR THOUGHTS

When you encounter a setback, such as not getting a callback after an audition, you may notice pessimistic self-talk, such as, "I am a terrible actor."

If you examine this thought, you will realize it is both extreme and inaccurate.

Maybe you are not good at improvisation or some other acting skill, but that does not mean you are a "terrible actor."

Your initial negative evaluation, "I am a terrible actor," could become, in the de-catastrophized version, "I am fine if I have a script in front of me, but I do not do well when I am asked to improvise."

This alternative is more specific about a particular type of acting you do not do well.

It is also more empowering by giving you a set of options.

You could decide that from now on, you will not go to auditions where strong improvisation skills are required.

Alternatively, you may decide to work on your improvisation skills to become more confident in this area, so you do better in these types of auditions.

To de-catastrophize your thoughts about yourself after a setback, it also helps to gain a sense of perspective.

Talk to your fellow actors about how they deal with negative self-talk when they encounter a setback.

You will realize you are not the only one battling negative self-talk and will find it easier to move on with a healthy mindset.

The better you feel about yourself, the higher your chances of success as you start pursuing new opportunities.

EXAMINE THE USEFULNESS OF YOUR THOUGHTS

There is no way to know why the setback happened–why you didn't get a callback after an audition, didn't get into drama school, or why a particular agent does not want to represent you.

On the other hand, blaming yourself for the setback impacts your state of mind; it is easier to overcome a setback if you do not see it as being your fault.

If there is no way to know the cause of the setback, and it is easier to overcome its effects if it was not your fault, why blame yourself?

There is a difference between observing your behavior so you can improve, and criticizing yourself.

If any of your self-criticisms do not include a clear path towards improving your chances of success, you are in fact harming your mental health instead of helping yourself do better next time.

When you realize you are criticizing yourself over something you did that might have led to the setback, ask yourself, will this self-criticism help you correct a specific mistake?

Will this self-talk help you improve, or will it undermine your self-confidence?

Make sure that any self-criticism is specific and action-oriented. This means you can do something about it next time you find yourself in a similar situation.

Beware of vague thoughts about your talent or looks, the kind of negative self-talk that undermines your self-confidence without offering a clear path towards improving things.

DISTRACT YOURSELF

Blaming yourself for setbacks is a difficult habit to change, so you may need to use the distraction tool more often when dealing with this aspect of pessimism.

The most effective way to distract yourself, if you obsess over how you could have done things differently, or your failings as an actor, is to focus on helping others.

Volunteer to do something that is meaningful to you and helps you shift your focus away from yourself.

For example, in *The Actor's Life*, Jenna Fischer talks about how fostering kittens helped her through her acting career struggles.

The more you can place your attention on others, the less you will think about the setback in a self-focused way.

After a while, you will feel better about the setback and will stop wondering whether you could have done anything to prevent it.

While going through the other tools, you might realize that you can and should change something about yourself as an actor.

For example, is there an aspect of the acting craft you would like to improve?

Do you need to work on your memorization process?

Are there skills (e.g., riding a horse, playing the piano) that would help you in auditioning for certain roles?

If you find something that is within your control to change and may improve your future chances, you can work on it using "deliberate practice."

Deliberate practice

Deliberate practice is a type of practice through which you can improve any aspect of your craft you would like to get better at.

For example, you could use deliberate practice to master a difficult accent, learn to play the piano, or develop strong improvisation skills.

The key to deliberate practice, as opposed to

practice in general, is that you must be extremely specific in isolating the exact elements you will focus on during your practice.

It is this laser-like focus that makes deliberate practice so effective.

When using deliberate practice, the goal you set is not about a particular outcome, but about the process of reaching that outcome.

Let's say you would like to improve your audition technique.

Most actors would set their sights on the final outcome: getting the part.

However, if you were to use deliberate practice, you would set a goal that focuses on the process of auditioning.

As an example, you could set the goal of using your breath to stay relaxed while waiting to be invited into the audition room.

You could be even more specific, such as deciding on a ratio of inbreaths to outbreaths, which would give you something to focus on while waiting.

Staying relaxed during the often-agonizing waiting period will allow you to perform better during your audition, bringing you closer to getting the part.

By setting a goal that is within your control, you are improving your chances of success, which is motivating and empowering.

Another important aspect of using this process is to evaluate how you did after every practice session.

This evaluation must be specific, so you can measure your progress, and non-judgmental.

The purpose of this evaluation is to understand what you did so you can do better next time, not to make yourself feel bad.

If you find things you could improve in the future, take note, and use what you learned to set an even more specific goal for the next practice session.

Deliberate practice takes a great deal of patience and perseverance, but working on any aspect of your craft in this way is guaranteed to help you improve.

This process is being used by top performers in a variety of disciplines and is well worth trying out if there is any skill or aspect of your craft you would like to get better at.

If you are interested in exploring how to apply deliberate practice as an actor, please read my book *Excellence for Actors*.

- It is easier to overcome a setback if you do not blame yourself for it.
- Pessimists go too far in taking responsibility for their mistakes and often fall into the rumination trap. This puts them at risk of developing long-term mental health problems.
- There is usually no evidence that the setback was caused by a mistake you made. Use your "greatest hits" to restore your self-confidence.
- If you identify something you could have done differently, use the growth mindset to reframe any negative self-judgment into a learning experience that will help you in the future.
- De-catastrophize your thoughts by making any self-criticism specific. This will provide you with self-knowledge about things to avoid in the future, or motivation to initiate change.
- Question the usefulness of your self-blaming thoughts. If they make you feel worse, and you have no evidence

that your mistakes caused the setback, there is no reason to allow such thoughts into your mind.

- You can distract yourself from self-blaming thoughts by placing your focus on helping others.
- You can also use deliberate practice to work on new skills or aspects of your craft that will improve your future chances of success.

CHAPTER 10

SETBACKS AS RITES OF PASSAGE

SETBACKS AND YOUR ACTING CAREER

Encountering setbacks is an integral part of life as an actor.

Your success does not depend on avoiding them, but on knowing how to recover from them when they happen, so you can get back into action quickly and easily.

The more skilled you become at navigating the difficult thoughts and feelings that arise following a setback, the more resilient you will be, and the more your chances of success will increase.

In this chapter, we will discuss different setbacks you may encounter over the course of your acting career, and how to approach each of these with an optimistic mindset.

NOT GETTING A CALLBACK

Not getting a callback is the most common type of setback for actors.

Of course, the chances of getting a callback are slim. And yet, the hope is always there, which is why it feels like a setback when it does not happen.

Yet it is worth acknowledging that not all such setbacks feel the same.

Not getting a callback after an audition when you didn't think you were right for the part, or you didn't perform at your best, is one thing.

You probably realized you were not a serious contender before you even left the audition room.

In such situations, simple tools, such as having a rejection target in mind, and saying to yourself, "I am getting one step closer to reaching my target," can work wonders for getting over the setback.

A more crushing scenario is when you felt well suited for the part, gave a great performance, maybe even detected some enthusiastic signs from the casting team, and then you didn't get a callback.

A setback of this kind is more difficult to take.

Indeed, research shows that near misses are more painful than attempts that do not come close.

Psychologists have speculated that such near-miss situations feel so upsetting because it is easy to imagine an alternative scenario, where everything went your way and you got the desired outcome.

If you find yourself in this situation, it is important to prevent the setback from dragging you down a slippery slope of pessimism and negative thinking.

Use all the tools you have learned in this book to challenge your pessimistic thoughts and replace them with empowering ones.

In addition, take some time to do things that make you feel good and bring you joy.

Give yourself the space to process the disappointment, but beware of the rumination trap.

Avoid replaying the situation over and over in your head, imagining how things could have turned out differently.

Talk about the situation with your actor friends, to remind yourself that you are not alone, as they will probably have similar stories.

Reading biographies, autobiographies, or

memoirs of actors who have achieved success can also be helpful at times like these.

Hearing about the near misses that successful actors had to endure along the way will remind you that these experiences are part of earning your stripes.

What matters is how you deal with these situations when they arise.

By reading this book, you are already taking proactive steps to deal with them in the best possible way.

NOT GETTING INTO DRAMA SCHOOL

Applying to drama school is a nerve-wracking process.

If you get rejected by all the drama schools you have applied to, you may need to wait a whole year before you can apply again.

Also, it is common for applicants to get rejected year after year.

What if this is not the first year you got rejected, maybe not even your second year trying?

Most applicants are young, with little experience of rejection and how to handle it, making this a difficult setback to overcome.

If you find yourself in this situation, take heart.

Some of the best-known actors got rejected by drama schools, and many had to try many times before getting in.

Take this year's rejections as a "Not yet," rather than a "Never."

Learning how to handle rejection well is a crucial life skill, especially for an actor.

In gaining experience dealing with such situations, you are laying a strong foundation for resilience throughout your entire acting career.

Use the waiting time to develop as a person and as an actor.

Are there skills you could pick up during this time, such as fencing, or riding a horse?

For example, in *The Monologue Audition*, Karen Kohlhaas advises actors to learn twenty monologues they can perform whenever needed.

Think how confident you would feel about monologue auditions if you had twenty monologues ready to go.

You would always have options available, an excellent asset during your next round of drama school applications.

GETTING REJECTED BY A POTENTIAL AGENT

The first thing to bear in mind if you get rejected by a potential agent is that this is not a reflection on your talent or ability as an actor.

Many other factors influence the agent's decision-making process.

If this agent is already representing someone similar to you, or doesn't send actors to the type of auditions that are right for you, it makes sense that they would reject you, and this is a good thing.

In the long run, this rejection may be a blessing in disguise.

Wouldn't you want to be represented by someone who is a good fit?

Best to think, "If this agent is not right for me, it means someone else is better suited to be my agent."

By opening yourself up to other potential agents, you will feel energized and motivated again, which will help you forget about this setback.

Getting fired as an actor is part of earning your stripes.

Many actors get fired, even well-known actors, and sometimes even after having achieved a high level of success.

But getting fired is painful, so it is best to have a few tools up your sleeve to recover from the hurt if this happens to you.

Take time to grieve. Getting fired feels like a loss, even if you didn't get on with the production team, or the project was not what you had envisaged when you came on board.

Don't gaslight yourself by thinking of all the things you could have done differently.

If there is something to learn from this experience, take note of it, but do not fall into the trap of endlessly analyzing the situation.

Ask yourself what you can do to make yourself feel better and do it. Look for fun things that nourish your soul.

Tell other actors you know and trust about what happened, as this will provide you with comfort and encouragement for the future.

Once you share your experience with fellow

actors, you will hear stories of others who got fired and how they dealt with it, which will help you feel less alone.

I also recommend watching Lisa Kudrow's speech at Vassar College about the time she got fired from *Frasier* and how she now views that situation many years later.

In hindsight, something that felt like the biggest disaster she had ever experienced turned out to be one of the luckiest things to have happened.

If you feel the need, explore the situation with the support of a therapist.

This will help you make peace with getting fired quicker than if you tried processing the hurt on your own.

Once you have taken some time to recover, figure out if it is time for a career reboot.

Opening yourself up to fresh opportunities will boost your dopamine and restore your energy.

Something else will come up that will suit you better, and you'll be glad things turned out the way they did.

And finally, think about how, in years to come, this experience will be part of the wisdom you can pass on to others.

When actors will sit around telling stories about how they got fired, you will have your own story to tell.

Your ability to recover and find new opportunities will help younger actors realize that getting fired may be the beginning of an exciting new chapter in their career.

RESILIENCE DAY-TO-DAY

Resilience is not always about overcoming a specific setback.

It is also about overcoming the quiet times in your acting career, when there are no auditions to go to and nothing interesting is happening.

How do you keep resilient during such times?

The best thing you can do is set up the kinds of circumstances that will make it easier to think optimistically.

This means identifying healthy ways to encourage your brain to release dopamine on a regular basis.

Doing this will counteract any pessimistic thoughts relating to the permanence aspect.

You should also ensure that you are living a

balanced life, instead of allowing your acting career to overshadow everything else.

This will make it easier to deal with the pervasiveness aspect of pessimism.

And to counteract the personalization aspect, engage in activities that direct your attention towards others and away from yourself.

In addition to setting up these optimism-friendly circumstances, it helps to keep in mind that creativity is cyclical, and that you are currently in the low-activity part of that cycle.

Use this time to recharge your energies and refuel your creativity, to be ready when things get busy once more.

By becoming skilled at using the quiet times in your acting career to recharge, you will make the most of any future opportunities that come your way.

CONCLUSION

As you start implementing the process and tools you have learned in this book, it is important to give yourself time and patience.

Learned optimism takes practice. If you are in the habit of thinking pessimistically when you encounter a setback in your acting career, this habit will require conscious effort to undo.

You won't often notice your pessimistic thoughts until you find yourself obsessing over them, by which time you will feel depleted of energy and motivation.

This is a natural thing to happen while changing your thought patterns, so do not beat yourself up over it.

Acknowledge your thoughts as they are and

use the tools in this book to get yourself energized and hopeful once again.

The growth mindset applies to learned optimism just as much as it applies to becoming better at anything else.

Becoming optimistic is about trial and error, and getting better over time, instead of trying to achieve perfection straight away.

The fact that you have read this book to the end and are taking proactive measures to increase your resilience is already a big step in the right direction.

The improvement in mental health you will achieve through applying everything you have learned in this book is well worth the effort.

If you can master responding to setbacks in a positive way, you will have a long and successful acting career.

Learning to use the tools in this book will put you miles ahead of where you are now.

You will no longer fear setbacks, because you will have a process to overcome the hurt and move on with a healthy mindset.

It is also worth pointing out that resilience is a life skill.

As you learn to use these tools in the context of

your acting career, you will also start applying them to other areas of your life.

These skills will not just make your acting career better–they will improve your whole life.

You are unique, so tailor the process of increasing your resilience to your own needs. Use the tools in this book as a starting point for developing your own process.

Please consider passing on this knowledge to any actor friends you see going through a difficult time because of career setbacks.

They will benefit and be happier for it, and you will become a beacon of strength and empowerment in their lives.

I wish you all the best with your acting career.

———

I would like to ask you for a small favor.

Reviews are the best way to spread the word about this book. If you have found this book helpful, it would mean a lot to me if you could leave a review.

Even if you write only a sentence or two, it will help. Thank you!

GET A FREE BOOK

If you want to improve your chances of success as an actor, psychology can help.

Psychology Tools for Actors teaches you ten simple yet powerful psychology tools to take your acting career to the next level.

Download for free when you sign up for the *Psychology for Actors* newsletter at:

www.psychologyforactors.com/newsletter

ABOUT THE AUTHOR

Alexa Ispas holds a PhD in psychology from the University of Edinburgh.

The books in her *Psychology for Actors Series* provide actors with proven psychology techniques to thrive and build a successful career.

If you'd like to stay in touch with Alexa and learn more psychological tools that are directly relevant to actors, please sign up for the *Psychology for Actors* newsletter. You will receive a short free book when you sign up.

You can sign up for the newsletter and receive your free book at:

www.psychologyforactors.com/newsletter

Memorization for Actors

Self-Confidence for Actors

Resilience for Actors

Motivation for Actors

Excellence for Actors

Success for Actors

For more information, please visit:

www.psychologyforactors.com